Saban's Power Rangers Megaforce

Power Rangers Samurai

Storybook

Collection

This edition published by Parragon Books Ltd in 2013

Parragon
Chartist House
15–17 Trim Street
Bath BA1 1HA, UK
www.parragon.com

Edited by Gemma Louise Lowe
Designed by Lucy Reynolds
Production by Joanne Knowlson

ISBN 978-1-4723-1992-0

Printed in China

Saban's Power Rangers Megaforce

Storybook Collection

Parragon

Bath • New York • Singapore • Hong Kong • Cologne • Delhi
Melbourne • Amsterdam • Johannesburg • Shenzhen

Contents

SABAN'S POWER RANGERS MEGAFORCE

Mega Mission

Thousands of miles above the Earth, the Warstar Battleship was headed for the planet it intended to destroy.

"What do you make of this planet, Earth?" Admiral Malkor asked Creepox, who had appeared on his viewing screen.

"Humans cannot match our insect strength. We'll swarm the planet and destroy them all," Creepox replied.

"I hope the humans don't cause a problem," said Vrak, a member of an insectoid royal family.

"Humans are only used to small, harmless insects on their planet. Wait until we land. We are the future. We will squash these humans and take this Earth for ourselves," Malkor said confidently.

On Earth, Emma Goodall and her camera were in the woods.

Emma went to take a picture of a butterfly when something in the distance caught her eye. Adjusting the zoom, Emma could hardly believe the creature she was

looking at. She hid behind a tree and hoped that whatever it was hadn't seen her.

Creepox made his way through the trees, brushing past the butterfly Emma had been watching a moment before.

"I smell a human," he growled.

Meanwhile, aware of the danger the Earth was facing, control panels sprang to life in an unused command centre. Two bright green eyes began to glow in the darkness – Gosei had been awakened from his slumber.

"Tensou, wake up! Aliens have already landed on Earth. It's time to assemble a new team of heroes," he instructed Tensou, his robotic companion. "Get me five kids with talent and attitude – and get them now!"

Moments later, Troy Burrows, Noah Carver, Jake Holling and Gia Morgan were teleported into the Command Centre.

"What just happened?" Jake asked. One moment he had been trying to buy Gia a frozen yoghurt and the next, she had vanished. Then, Noah had disappeared ... and now Jake was in this weird place, too!

"I'm not sure. But it was scientifically impossible ... and awesome!" said Noah, looking at all the amazing technology that surrounded them.

"How'd we end up here?" wondered Troy. He had been practising some of his martial-arts moves when he had just disappeared off the rooftop he had been standing on.

"Just where is here?" asked Gia.

A booming voice sounded around the Command Centre.

"Welcome, humans!" said a voice as a great face lit up the room. "I am Gosei. Your lives are about to change. My mentor, Zordon, placed me here to be guardian of this planet. I am of the Earth and I embody its great and mystical powers. I only awaken when the Earth is under a significant threat. The Earth needs you."

"What are you talking about?" enquired Gia.

"Aliens have already landed and you have been chosen to protect Earth," Gosei continued. Just then, Emma transported into the Command Centre.

"You've got to be kidding me," laughed Jake.

"He's not kidding," declared Emma, walking over and showing them the picture of Creepox she had taken in the woods.

"This can't be real," said Gia.

"Your scepticism is healthy," Gosei told her, "but this is all too real. You have been carefully selected to form a team in the long tradition of Power Rangers. You shall protect the Earth as MEGAFORCE."

As the teens watched images of themselves flashed up on the monitors around the Command Centre. Gosei addressed them one by one.

"Emma, you are a great BMX biker and you truly care about the environment. You shall soar up from the flames like a phoenix and be the Pink Ranger.

"Noah, your thirst for knowledge is unequalled. As the Blue Ranger your attacks will bite with the force of a shark.

"Jake, I am making you the Black Ranger who will fight with the stealth of a snake.

"Gia, you pursue excellence with the ferocity of a tiger. You will be the Yellow Ranger.

"Last, but not least, Troy. You shall be the Red Ranger – the dragon and team leader."

"There must be some mistake," said Troy. "I'm new in town." Today had been his first day at the school.

"There is no mistake," Gosei assured him. "You have been chosen because of your skills and character."

Suddenly, strange objects that looked like Gosei appeared in the hands of the new Rangers.

"Those are your Mega Morphers and Power Cards," Gosei explained. "With them you will morph into Mega Rangers. Power Cards will give you access to special weapons and abilities, and you shall command mighty machines called Megazords."

"All this tech," marvelled Noah. "How do we use it?"

"All will be revealed in time," Gosei assured him.

"If the Earth is under attack and you think we're the ones to protect it, we're in," said Troy.

"Your mission starts now! Believe in yourselves!" Gosei encouraged them.

Suddenly, the team felt the same energy pulse that had brought them to the Command Centre and then found themselves at the edge of town.

"Look!" called Emma. The others turned to see green spheres of energy that became toxic foot soldiers called Loogies.

"They're headed for the city!" shouted Troy. "We have to stop them!"

But the Loogies quickly spotted the group of teens and sprang an attack. The startled team were instantly surrounded.

Acting quickly, Troy launched an attack to take down two Loogies.

"Come on, let's do this!" Troy said encouragingly.

Nearby, Gia threw some quick punches on a few of the toxic aliens.

Meanwhile, Emma flashed her camera at one of the Loogies, blinding him before kicking him to the ground. Jake saw another Loogie coming towards him. Thinking quickly, he threw his football into the air and blasted it towards the Loogie, knocking it off its feet.

However, it wasn't long before most of the teens were overpowered.

"This isn't good," cried Jake. There is only so much that normal kids can do against alien monsters.

"They're closing in on us!" said Gia.

"Gosei said these Morphers will give us power. Let's use them," Troy told the others. "Follow my lead! It's morphing time!"

They all pulled out their Power Cards and placed them into the Morphers.

"Go, Go Megaforce!" they all shouted together.

"Megaforce Red!" Troy called out as he went through the morphing sequence that turned him into the Red Ranger.

The other teens all followed suit and morphed into Megaforce Rangers.
"Megaforce Blue!" cried Noah.
"Megaforce Black!" cried Jake.
"Megaforce Pink!" cried Emma.
"Megaforce Yellow!" cried Gia.
"Earth's defenders never surrender!" they shouted together.
Glancing at each other, the Rangers quickly leapt into action.

"It's time for our new weapons," said Yellow Ranger as she pulled out her weapon card and placed it into her Morpher.

Gosei's voice boomed. "Summon battle gear!"

"Tiger Claw!" shouted Yellow Ranger.

The other Rangers all summoned their own weapons.

"Awesome!" yelled Blue Ranger.

"It's like I was born to do this," Black Ranger agreed as the signal on their Morphers began to buzz.

"Good job, but there's no time to celebrate," Red Ranger told the others. "Let's take the fight to them, guys!"

In the distance the team could see the terror being unleashed by the Loogies. People were running everywhere, desperate to escape. The aliens were throwing them to the ground, smashing up cars and firing their weapons at the crowd.

As the Yellow and Black Rangers worked together, swinging their weapons down to the pavement to launch a Mega Quake, they didn't realize that more Foot Soldiers had lined up behind them.

"Shark Bow!" shouted Noah, blasting the aliens and landing beside his friends. "Loving this Bowgun!" Almost immediately, more Loogies arrived, severely outnumbering the Rangers.

"Phoenix Shot!" cried Pink Ranger as she swooped in, blasting more of the aliens. "Did you see that? I can fly!"

After a moment, more Loogies appeared and formed a circle around the Rangers. "Uh-oh," said Black Ranger.
"We need Troy."

Just then, a red tornado whipped through the circle of Loogies, before landing and transforming into the Red Ranger.

"Whoa, these powers are amazing!" Red Ranger said.

"Nice moves!" said Yellow Ranger. "Any idea how to get out of this?"

"Look sharp!" warned Red Ranger as the Megaforce team turned to face yet more Loogies.

On the bridge of the Warstar, Admiral Malkor was not happy.

"Pesky humans! They dare to fight back? It'll be our pleasure to destroy them all."

"If I were you," suggested Vrak, "I'd test these Rangers with a real monster."

"Scaraba, the rock beetle. I summon you to battle!" Malkor announced.

A bronze beetle-like alien appeared. "Reporting for duty, sir. There's no thug like a bug!" he said.

Malkor gave him his instructions and sent the creature to destroy the humans – especially the Megaforce Rangers.

"Run, humans! Run!" cried Scaraba. He began to chase the civilians, while running on top of a giant ball of rubble. The terrified people ran for their lives.

"Hey, monster," called Black Ranger, mockingly. "Leave those folks alone!"

"You mean me?" replied Scaraba.

"You can scare them," said Red Ranger, walking towards Scaraba, "But we are not afraid." The Megaforce Rangers formed a line. "We'll protect the Earth," promised Red Ranger. "No matter what it takes."

Scaraba called up a line of Loogies, who all aimed their weapons at the Rangers.

"Rangers," called Gosei, "It's time to call upon your Blasters."

"Let's do it!" called Blue Ranger.

The team all pulled out their Blaster Cards and slotted them into their Morphers. "Blasters, activate!" they shouted together.

The Rangers' Blasters appeared in the their hands and they aimed them towards the Loogies.

"OK, let's fry these Loogies!" called Yellow Ranger.

"It's on!" roared Red Ranger.

"Shark Blast!" shouted Blue Ranger as he aimed his Blaster at a Loogie.

"Dragon Blast!" screamed Red Ranger.

Working together as a team, the Megaforce soon defeated all the Loogies.

"I'll crush you!" called Scaraba as he rolled towards them on the rubble ball.

The Rangers all aimed their Blasters at the ball and it exploded.

"You punks are megaforcing me to lose my lunch!" wailed a frustrated Scaraba.

"Let's call on the Mega Weapons!" said Red Ranger.

Once again, the Rangers each pulled a card from their belt and placed it into their Morphers. "Weapons, activate!" they called together.

"Now it's time to show our true Mega Power!" shouted Red Ranger.

The symbols on the Rangers' chests began to glow as they combined their special weapons together to form the Megaforce Blaster.

Red Ranger held up the Megaforce Blaster, while the others gathered round him.

"Whoa!" said Scaraba, knowing this was not going to be good for him.

The Pink and Red Rangers lifted their Power Cards together and placed them on the Megaforce Blaster.

"Sky Power, energize!"

"Land Power, energize!" called Black and Yellow Rangers together.

"Sea Power, energize!" added

Blue Ranger, placing his own card on to the Megaforce Blaster.

"Dynamic victory charge!" they called together.

A great energy pulse fired from the weapon, engulfing Scaraba in a magical glow, before sending him flying off into the distance.

"Mega Rangers," said Red Ranger, "that's a mega win!"

"Megaforce!" they all shouted together.

"Congratulations on a job well done," said Gosei.

"But we were just lucky this time," replied a worried Noah.

"Luck had nothing to do with it," Gosei assured them. "You rose to the occasion and unlocked your powers. Do not doubt yourselves. You were chosen and for good reason. This morning you were regular kids, leading normal lives. But now you must master your new powers and lead extraordinary lives."

"We're a force to be reckoned with!" agreed Troy.

SABAN'S POWER RANGERS MEGAFORCE

He Blasted Me with Science

On the bridge of the Warstar, hovering above Earth, Admiral Malkor and his team were plotting ways to ensure humanity's destruction.

"I believe we should study these humans and learn their weaknesses," Vrak suggested.

"I see," said the admiral, taking this idea onboard and thinking of a way to make it work. "Yuffo," he called. "I have need of your scientific skills."

A flying saucer whirled into the room and transformed into a beetle-like monster with a large spiny round shell on his back.

"An honour, sir," Yuffo answered.

"I want you to find the humans' weaknesses," Malkor instructed. "Capture as many as you need."

Meanwhile, back on Earth, Jake Holling and Gia Morgan were walking home through a wooded park when Gia spotted something odd over Jake's shoulder – a flying saucer!

Instantly, Gia's experience as a Ranger alerted her to the danger and she got her Morpher out of her backpack.

"Whoa!" Jake saw the saucer as well. It split into five saucers which all began to fly across the park.

The saucers swooped low over a group of people and dropped a net over them. The people were dragged across the park in the net, before the saucers reformed into Yuffo.

Gia and Jake drew their Morphers at once.

"Go, Go Megaforce!" they shouted as they morphed into the Yellow and Black Rangers.

"Snake Blast!" roared Black Ranger.

"Tiger Blast!" cried Yellow Ranger, as they both fired at Yuffo with their Mega Blasters.

"Mega Rangers, you're the perfect specimens for my research programme!" Yuffo told them happily.

"Let those people go!" Black Ranger demanded.

"I'm really very sorry, but I can't allow you to interfere with my experiment. Unless you're willing to join these volunteers."

"That would be a no! I'm very sorry, but this experiment is over," said Yellow Ranger.

Yuffo summoned a squad of Loogies, who leapt into battle with the Rangers.

"We can take 'em," Black Ranger assured Yellow Ranger.

The Rangers did well at first, but were quickly overwhelmed by the number of Loogies.

"On second thought, maybe we could use some back-up," Black Ranger suggested.

"I'm calling the others," Yellow Ranger agreed, dispatching a Loogie with her Tiger Claw and using her Morpher to call the others at the same time.

Moments later, the Red Ranger joined the fight, Blaster firing.

"Heads up!" he called as he dived through the air into the battle. "Got your back!"

"What a magnificent sight! Three Power Rangers! What luck! Let's start my experiment right now!" said Yuffo, blasting the Rangers with a pulse of energy.

The Rangers fell to the ground, stunned, but just as suddenly Yuffo was knocked off his feet by the Pink Ranger, firing from a nearby ridge.

"We don't let injury stop us!" said Pink Ranger as she leapt down and helped the others to their feet.

"He keeps talking about some experiment," said Red Ranger, puzzled.

"He thinks he's a scientist," explained Black Ranger.

"He probably wants to see what weapons work best on humans," reasoned Pink Ranger.

"That's not gonna happen!" said Red Ranger, defiantly.

As Yuffo called in more Loogies, the four Rangers rushed to face them with their special weapons.

"Snake Axe!"

"Tiger Claw!"

"Phoenix Shot!"

"Dragon Sword!"

"Saucer Wave," countered Yuffo, launching a fleet of mini saucers, which knocked the Ranger to the ground again.

"Perhaps we'll test their resistance to fire!" suggested Yuffo, approaching the Rangers. "At this rate, destroying the human race will be child's play."

"I've got a shock for you," announced the Blue Ranger as he leapt at the alien, his weapon blazing.

Yuffo was slammed backwards by the force of the blow and Blue Ranger ran over to help his friends to their feet. "See, Jake, I told you flying saucers were real!"

"I think it's time to take this guy down," said Yellow Ranger.

The Rangers all began their power-up sequence.

"Earth's defenders never surrender!" shouted Red Ranger.

"Power Rangers Megaforce!" they all cried together.

"No!" screamed Yuffo as Black and Red Rangers went first. Their attack was quickly followed by blasts from the Pink and Yellow Rangers. Finally, Blue Ranger grabbed the alien and plunged him into the sea.

After a few blasts from Blue Ranger's Shark Bowgun, Yuffo was thrown back on to the beach.

“Let’s try an experiment of our own,” suggested Blue Ranger.

The Rangers locked their weapons together to form the Megaforce Blaster, then placed their cards into it.

“Sky Power, energize!” said the Red and Pink Rangers.

“Land Power, energize!” cried the Yellow and Black Rangers.

“Sea Power, energize!” shouted Blue Ranger, placing the final card.

“Dynamic victory charge!” they called as they fired the Megaforce Blaster at Yuffo.

As they did, Yuffo’s nets, which were holding the humans captive, disappeared in a flash of light.

On the Warstar bridge, Admiral Malkor was furious. The admiral turned to his companion. "Vrak," he said. "Unleash your pets."

Vrak smiled as a flock of robotic Zombats hovered around him.

"Zombats, go!" he instructed as the flying creatures hurried off.

Arriving on Earth the Zombats clamped themselves to Yuffo's body.
He began to glow and shake as he transformed into Giant Yuffo!

"How is that possible?" exclaimed Yellow Ranger.

"The experiment continues," Giant Yuffo chuckled.

He tried to squash the Rangers with an enormous fist, but they deftly managed to dodge the attack.

"You move pretty fast for such tiny little creatures," taunted Giant Yuffo.

"Hear me, Rangers," Gosei's voice called to them. "There are even greater powers at your command, but controlling them requires great skill and discipline."

"We're ready, Gosei; we have to be," Red Ranger assured him.

"Then take these Power Cards and use them wisely."

At once the Rangers' belt buckles began to glow. Blue Ranger pulled out a blank card and before his eyes an image of the Shark Zord appeared on it.

"They're Zords!" he told the others.

"Rangers, we're back in the fight," said Red Ranger.

The Rangers all put their new cards into the Morphers and called their Zords.

"Gosei Dragon, activate," called Red Ranger. The other Rangers followed suit.

"Gosei Phoenix, activate."

"Gosei Shark, activate."

"Gosei Tiger, activate."

"Gosei Snake, activate."

Gosei's voice rang out, "Summon Zords!"

Many miles away on Tiki Island, stone casing fell from the ancient Zords. Giant animal heads blasted off and flew through the air.

The Dragon Zord flew over the nose of an airliner to become the Dragon Mechazord.

The Phoenix Zord combined with a jet fighter to create the Phoenix Mechazord.

The Snake Zord joined with a bullet train to form the Snake Mechazord.

The Tiger Zord melded with a bulldozer to create the Tiger Mechazord, and the Shark Zord dived deep to a submarine and became the Shark Mechazord.

The Rangers were stunned as their new Mechazords whirled into view.

"Gosei told us the Earth would help us protect it with mighty machines," said Blue Ranger.

"I hope they run on biofuel!" said Pink Ranger.

"No, Emma, they run on us. Our courage, our strength, that's what gives them power. To our Mechazords!" instructed Red Ranger.

The Rangers all leapt high into the air and landed in their respective Mechazord's cockpits. They locked their Morphers into the consoles and prepared for battle.

Giant Yuffo split himself into a cluster of saucers, which took off in every direction, scattering the Rangers in many directions as they tried to follow them.

The Dragon Mechazord, piloted by Red Ranger, flew after one group of saucers, but they began pumping out clouds of black smoke. Red Ranger was flying blind, but he still managed to take a couple of the saucers down.

Once he broke free of the smoke, Red Ranger saw a couple more saucers right on Pink Ranger's tail, but he couldn't get into firing position. She flew into a tunnel and was followed by the saucers. Pink Ranger expertly piloted the Phoenix Mechazord through the tunnel and out the other side, but found herself squinting in the midday sun.

"I can't see!" she cried.

"Just trust me!" said Red Ranger as he fired a volley of missiles that blasted her pursuers away.

The shattered saucers fell into the ocean and the Shark Mechazord jumped out of the water like a dolphin, before diving back down into the ocean's depths to take on its own saucers.

"This is incredible! Such advanced technology! We have target-lock and fire!" Blue Ranger announced as two torpedoes launched and made a direct hit with the saucers. "Score two for the hi-tech approach!"

Another saucer tried to pull the Shark Mechazord into a whirlpool. Blue Ranger struggled with the controls for a second before the Shark Mechazord leapt out of the water, destroying the third saucer with its powerful jaws.

"Woohoo!" shouted Blue Ranger.

On the shore, the Tiger Mechazord burst through the hillside chasing more saucers.

"Let's see what this cat can do!" exclaimed Yellow Ranger. "A girl could get used to this kind of power."

The Snake Mechazord pulled up alongside.

"I'll take 'em down!" Black Ranger told Yellow Ranger as the Snake Mechazord wound its way through the saucers, dodging their fire until it was in front of them.

The saucers slammed into the Snake Mechazord's armoured hide and bounced off – straight towards the waiting Tiger Mechazord. The Tiger Mechazord grabbed the saucers in its jaws and hurled them into the distance, where they hit the ground and exploded.

After the Rangers had hunted down the rest of the saucers, only one remained, but it transformed back into Giant Yuffo. It was as if they were back where they had started!

"Can this guy be beat?" Red Ranger asked in frustration. "He's indestructible!"

"Let's resume our experiment, shall we?" asked Giant Yuffo.

The voice of Gosei communicated with his team once more. "Rangers, you must combine your Mechazords, just as you combined your weapons. The power you can release as a team is unequal. Form the Megazord!"

"You heard him," said Red Ranger. "Form the Gosei Great Megazord!"

The Rangers each reached into their belts and pulled out new cards, which transformed to show the Gosei Great Megazord. As they placed the cards into their Morphers, the transformation began....

The Snake Mechazord curled its tail rround to connect to the Tiger Mechazord. Both Mechazords then bent upwards, forming a pair of towering legs.

The Dragon Mechazord perched carefully on top of this, with the Phoenix Mechazord and the Shark Mechazord attaching to either side of it, forming arms. Finally, the Megazord's head rotated up.

All five Rangers were teleported to the new five-station cockpit.

"Gosei Great Megazord, ready!" they called in unison.

"Whoa, this thing is sick!" exclaimed Black Ranger.

"Let's finish this guy for good!" said Red Ranger, and they used the controls to walk the Megazord into battle.

Giant Yuffo fired an energy beam at the Megazord, but missed.

The Megazord continued towards Yuffo, drawing its Dragon Sword. It swung the sword, but the blows seemed to have little effect.

The Megazord then launched all five Zords at Giant Yuffo. Though detached from the Megazord's body, the heads were still controlled remotely by the Rangers. A left hook from the Megazord became a rocket-powered punch from the Phoenix Zord. The Zords swirled round Yuffo's body, punishing him mercilessly, before combining once more.

"Argh, my aching head!" Yuffo cried.

"Quickly, Rangers," commanded Gosei. "Use the Victory Charge Card."

"Let's finish this!" cried Red Ranger. "For planet Earth!"

"Let's finish him! Victory Charge!" shouted the Rangers.

"I don't like this card game!" whined Yuffo.

"Mega Strike!" shouted the Rangers.

The Megazord delivered a powerful finishing move and Yuffo exploded in a flash of light.

In the cockpit, the Rangers celebrated. Red Ranger punched his fist into the air. "Now that's a mega win!"

木

I've Got a Spell on Blue

Kevin, the Blue Ranger, was practising his sword skills with Jayden, the Red Ranger, one morning at the Shiba House.

"Wow! Kevin's technique is really good," said Mia.

"They're both so good, I hate to think what would happen if they had to fight each other," added Mike.

"That would NEVER happen," said Emily.

Meanwhile, deep down in the Netherworld, Deker was talking to Master Xandred.

"I want to go after the Red Ranger, the leader of the Samurai Rangers," said Deker.

"Do what you will," snarled Master Xandred. "My head is pounding. I can only deal with one headache at a time."

Deker knew that his master was still suffering from when the last Red Ranger had sealed him down in the Netherworld. It would be some time before he fully recovered his strength. With Master Xandred's permission, Deker left to continue his quest.

Just as Deker was leaving, a Nighlok named Madimot came aboard Master Xandred's ship, boasting that he was in control of the Red Ranger's long-lost TigerZord. When the earth had cracked open and the last Red Ranger had sealed Master Xandred in the Netherworld, the TigerZord fell in the crevice, too. Madimot saved it and used his mind-control powers to make the Zord his pet. Now he planned to turn the TigerZord against the Rangers.

As Madimot entered our world, the Gap Sensor at the Shiba House lit up to alert the Samurai Rangers.

In a flash, the Rangers were ready to confront him, but were amazed to see that he had the powerful TigerZord under his power.

The Rangers knew they must get the TigerZord back, but Madimot shot out a mind-controlling ray at the Rangers.

"Everyone duck!" yelled the Red Ranger.

But the Green Ranger was too slow and the ray was coming right at him. Bravely, the Blue Ranger pushed the Green Ranger out of the way and the ray hit him instead. The Blue Ranger was now under Madimot's evil control and started to fight his fellow Rangers. Madimot sent a mind-control blast towards the Red Ranger, who countered the ray with his special Resist Disc.

Although the Rangers fought well, Madimot had both the Blue Ranger and the TigerZord on his side, and managed to overpower the Green, Yellow and Pink Rangers. The Red Ranger had no choice but to use his powers to transport the others to safety, leaving the Blue Ranger and the TigerZord with Madimot. But Madimot was drying out and needed to get back to the Sanzu River for a soak that would recharge his power.

"You wait here until I get back," he said as he ordered the Blue Ranger to stay with the TigerZord.

While Madimot was busy in the Netherworld, Deker was in our world. Being only half Nighlok, he was not so interested in harming humans – instead his wish was to fight the ultimate duel. Fighting the Red Ranger would fulfil that desire, and Deker needed to keep tabs on his future opponent, for one day they would meet in battle.

Meanwhile, Madimot couldn't resist having some fun with the Blue Ranger, who was still in his power. Together, they were causing mayhem at a local construction site. Not wanting to endanger his fellow Rangers, Jayden set off to face Madimot and the Blue Ranger alone. When Mia, Mike and Emily realized this, they followed him, knowing that it was their duty to help.

Meanwhile, Jayden was facing an impossible choice – if he didn't fight the Blue Ranger, Madimot would order the Blue Ranger to turn his sword on himself. Shortly after the other Rangers arrived, Jayden morphed into the Red Ranger and began his unwilling battle with the Blue Ranger.

As the Rangers watched the fight, they were unaware that a nearby stranger was Deker in human form. After watching the Red Ranger fight, Deker was more certain than ever that the Red Ranger was the right opponent for the ultimate duel.

As the Red Ranger fought, he tried to get close enough to the Blue Ranger to use the Resist Disc to break Madimot's spell. Attaching it to his Spin Sword, he freed him from the Nighlok's control.

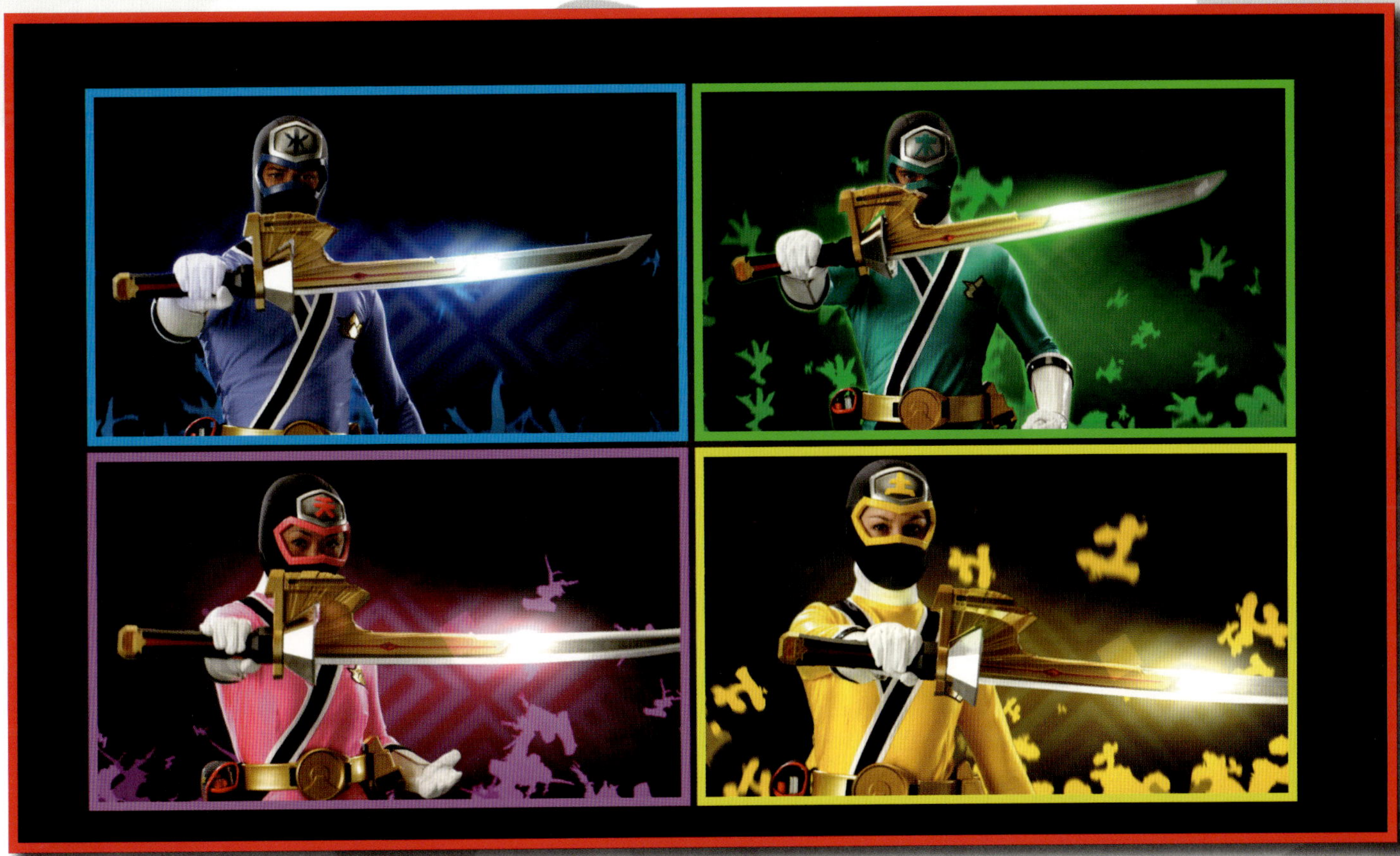

Now that all the Rangers were a team again, they morphed and sprang into action to help battle Madimot.

"You guys take care of the Nighlok. I'll handle the TigerZord," said the Red Ranger.

While the others raced off to battle Madimot, the Red Ranger prepared to face the TigerZord.

"LionZord! MegaMode Power!" he yelled as he wrote the magic Kanji Symbol that would summon his Zord.

As soon as he was in the cockpit, the TigerZord charged at the LionZord with its claws spinning. This was tougher than the Red Ranger had thought, but as soon as he was able to knock down the TigerZord, the Red Ranger leaped into the Zord and placed the Resist Disc in the control panel.

"TigerZord! Resist Power!" he yelled, and Madimot's power was lifted once again.

The TigerZord was back where it belonged.

With the whole team against him, Madimot was soon defeated – but every Nighlok has a second life as a MegaMonster!

The Red Ranger and the TigerZord began battling Madimot while the other Rangers went into MegaMode, ready to help him.

After they all morphed into MegaMode, the Red Ranger wrote the magic Kanji Symbol for ‘combination’ and the five Zords combined to form the massive Megazord.

“Samurai Megazord! We are united!” shouted the Rangers together.

“Samurai Artillery!” yelled the Red Ranger, and the TigerZord combined with the Megazord.

“Tiger Drill Megazord! Armed for battle!” shouted all the Rangers together in the Megazord cockpit.

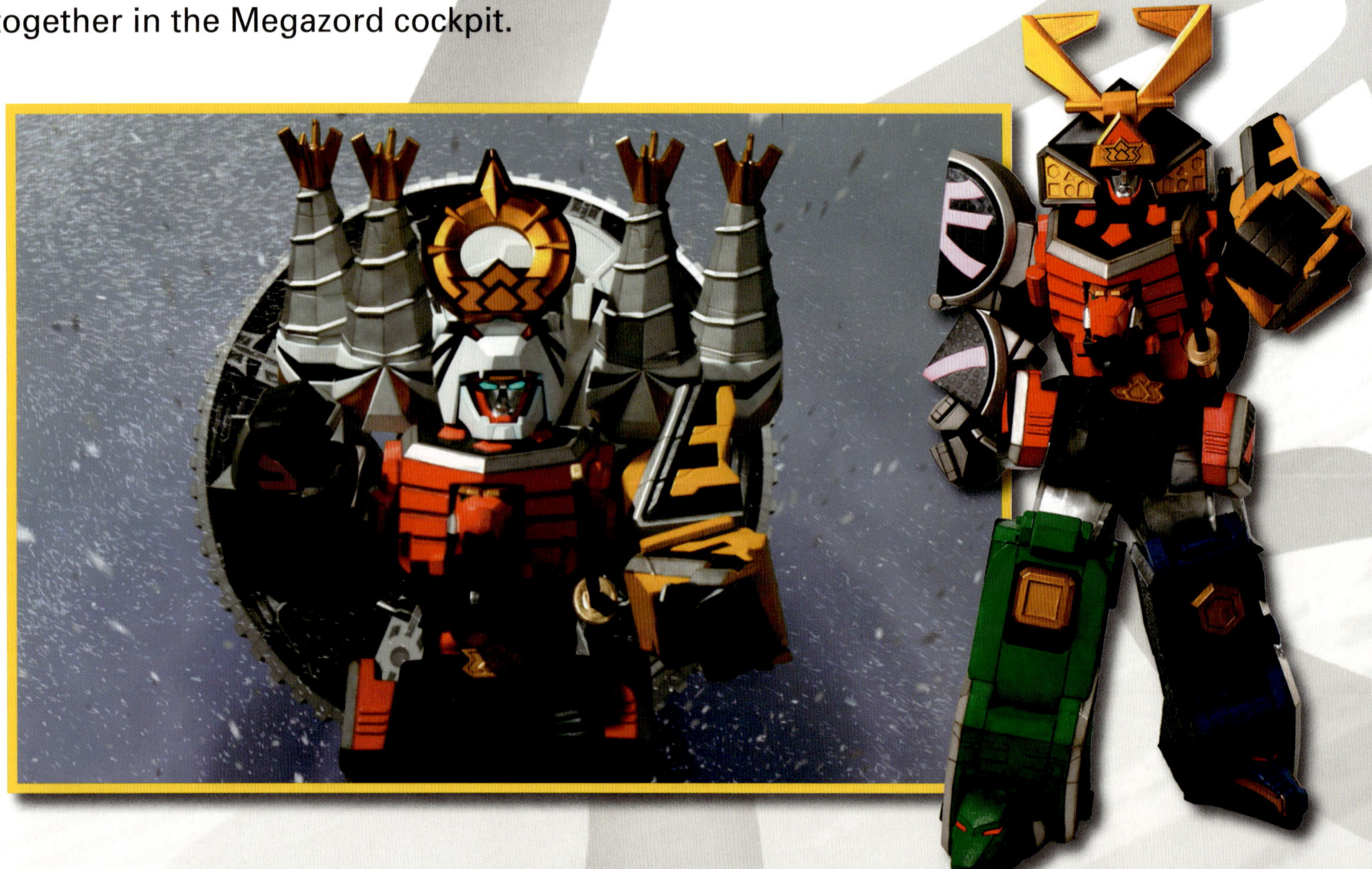

The Tiger Drill Megazord and Madimot battled fiercely. Even Madimot's powerful shield was no match for the Tiger Drill, and before long Madimot was defeated for good.

"Samurai Rangers, victory is ours!" said the Red Ranger triumphantly.

Another battle against a Nighlok had been won, but the Red Ranger knew there would be more to come. A Samurai Ranger is always on guard!

Jayden's Challenge

Jayden, the Red Ranger, is the only Ranger with the power to seal Master Xandred and the Nighlok back in the Netherworld. Master Xandred and the Nighlok monsters were getting stronger by the day.

The Samurai Rangers would have lost their last battle with Robtish if it hadn't been for the half-human Nighlok, Deker, stepping in to save the Red Ranger. He wanted to save the Red Ranger for himself, believing it was his destiny to battle Jayden in the ultimate duel. The Samurai Rangers had been wounded in their last battle and Jayden didn't want to put them in any more danger. He felt he must defeat the Nighlok alone.

When Master Xandred discovered how Deker had saved the Red Ranger, he was furious and went with his Moogers to destroy Deker. But Deker, who was more powerful than Master Xandred had realized, managed to get away.

"This is far from over!" roared Master Xandred as Deker made his escape.

Robtish was still angry with Deker, too. He decided to squirm his way through a gap back into our world to have another go at defeating the Red Ranger.

Meanwhile, Jayden was by himself walking around the city. He watched some children playing in the park.

"This is the way life should be," he thought to himself. "Happy and carefree, with no monsters to worry about."

All of a sudden, Robtish appeared with a horde of Moogers.

"Run away, kids!" yelled Jayden, as he prepared to fight.

Back at the Shiba House, the other Rangers were worried about Jayden.

"Jayden doesn't want to put you in any more danger," explained Mentor Ji to the other Rangers. "This is something he wants to do alone."

However, when the Gap Sensor went off, they wanted to go and help Jayden.

"We're in this together," said Mia. "We can't let Jayden do this by himself."

The other Rangers agreed and, together, they raced off to help.

When they arrived on the scene, the Rangers told Jayden they were in this together.

"Somebody's got to stop the Nighlok," Jayden told his friends, "and I'm glad it's us!"

"Rangers together! Samurai forever!" chanted the team as they morphed into Samurai Rangers, ready to fight.

Working as a team, the Rangers soon defeated the Moogers before facing off against Robtish.

Now the battle was between Robtish and the Samurai Rangers. Using his Samurai senses, the Red Ranger was able to predict Robtish's next move. He warned the Rangers to be ready for Robtish to send out a shock wave. While the Rangers deflected the wave, Jayden was getting ready with a trick of his own.

"Say hello to my Fire Smasher!" the Red Ranger shouted.

"Five Disc Tiger Cannon – Rangers, lend me your discs!" he called to the others.

With their combined powers, the Samurai Rangers overcame Robtish. However, within seconds, Robtish came back to fight some more, this time as a MegaMonster.

"Lion FoldingZord! Turtle FoldingZord! Dragon FoldingZord! Bear FoldingZord! Ape FoldingZord!" cried out each of the Rangers in turn.

"MegaMode Power!" they all shouted together.

In MegaMode, the Rangers were very powerful, but they were never stronger than when they worked as a team.

"Zords, combine!" they commanded in unison.

The five Zords locked together to form the awesome Megazord. Now the Samurai Rangers felt ready for anything. But they were shocked about the MegaMonster's next trick – flying Moogers!

"Perhaps the Samurai Battlewing could help?" suggested the Green Ranger.

But the Blue Ranger had another idea.

"What if we combine the Samurai Battlewing with the Megazord?" he said.

This was an idea that the Blue Ranger had been working on for a while, and he had some diagrams to show how it could work.

"First, we must combine the TigerZord, the BeetleZord and the SwordfishZord to create the Samurai Battlewing," said the Blue Ranger as he sprang into action.

The Samurai Battlewing blasted one shot at Robtish to distract him while it split into pieces and attached itself to the Megazord.

It was now a Battlewing Megazord that Robtish and his flying Moogers had to face.

Now that the Megazord could fly, it wasn't long before the flying Moogers were wiped out.

"Bye, bye, birdies!" laughed the Yellow Ranger.

It was just Robtish that the Rangers had to battle.

"Looks like we saved the worst for last," said the Red Ranger, as they prepared to fight.

Robtish was very powerful, but the Rangers launched an aerial attack on him.

"Let's fly up so we can take him down," said the Blue Ranger.

The Samurai Rangers activated their Mega Blades, and from way up in the air they dived down on the MegaMonster. With one great slash of their mighty blade, Robtish was finally defeated.

水 水 水

"Samurai Rangers, victory is ours!" said the Red Ranger proudly.

The Red Ranger knew there was still a lot of work left to do before the Nighlok were defeated, but he was very glad he had his team there to help him do it.

Unexpected Arrival

A young man on a mission was making his way into town one morning. Where he was heading was a mystery, but one that would soon be revealed.

At the Shiba House, the Gap Sensor was flashing. The Rangers hurried off, ready to fight whatever evil awaited them. However, when they got to where the Sensor had been set off, there wasn't a Nighlok in sight.

"Perhaps the Gap Sensor isn't working," suggested Kevin.

But when they checked it, they found it was working fine. The Rangers went back to the Shiba House, feeling puzzled. But Jayden felt sure he could sense a presence, even though none of the other Rangers could.

Deep down in the dark Netherworld, a Nighlok named Vulpes was up to no good. With his special inter-dimensional mirror, he had been spying on Jayden to try and find out his secret Sealing Symbol – the magic symbol that he would use one day to seal Master Xandred and the Nighlok monsters back in the Netherworld for good.

Back at the Shiba House, there was a loud swishing sound, followed by a thud as something hit the wall of the Shiba House. The Rangers rushed outside to see what it was. They found an arrow stuck in the wall with a message written in black ink attached. It said SEE YOU SOON! None of the Rangers knew what this meant or who could have sent it, although Mike noticed that the message smelled of fish.

Jayden was still sure that something had invaded their house, even though it was protected from the Nighlok by magic Power Symbols.

"Are you sure you're not imagining things?" asked Mia.

But Mentor Ji had always taught Jayden to trust his instincts, so that was what he intended to do. He felt as if somebody was watching him all the time and he knew things weren't right. The only time the feeling stopped was when he was near water. This gave Jayden an idea.

Later that day, Mike, Mia, Emily and Kevin went out to check the area where the Gap Sensor had gone off. They were still worried that something might be wrong. While they were out, they noticed a young man selling fish. He was handing out leaflets, and Emily noticed that the writing on them matched the writing on the mysterious note. When they questioned the young man, he was shocked. He realized who he was talking with.

"No, you're going to ruin my big moment," he said as he ran away.

Just then, Mike got a call from Mentor Ji. He told them that Jayden had gone to Spring Valley on his own. Kevin and Mia decided to follow Jayden, leaving Mike and Emily to chase after the mysterious fish seller.

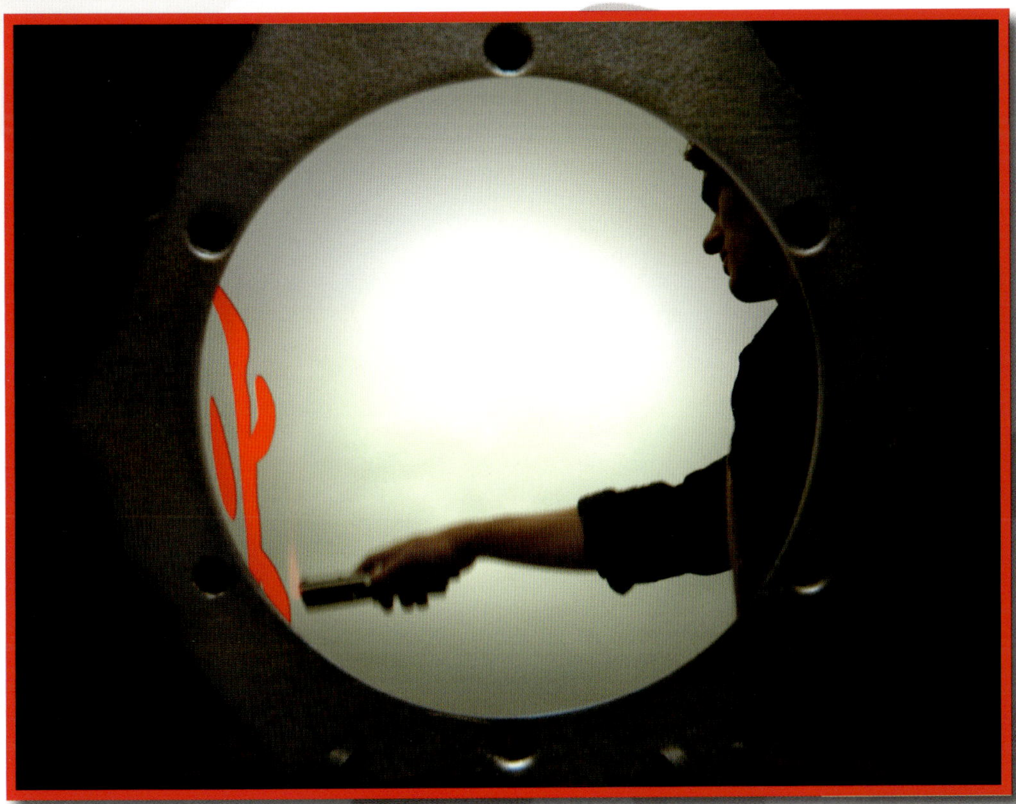

Down in the Netherworld, Vulpes was watching Jayden through his magic mirror. Jayden was standing by a lake and practising his Sealing Symbol. Vulpes felt sure he would soon learn the secret of the magic Sealing Symbol. However, as he watched, smoke filled the mirror, clouding Vulpes' view. When the smoke cleared, Jayden was nowhere to be seen. Vulpes was furious and decided to challenge Jayden face to face.

Meanwhile, Emily and Mike were still chasing the fish man, who was really giving them the runaround. They stopped to catch their breath, but couldn't see the mysterious man anywhere.

When Vulpes arrived at Spring Valley the Red Ranger sprang at the Nighlok from out of the sacred Spring Valley waters. Vulpes didn't see him coming, and the Red Ranger grabbed the magic mirror from Vulpes.

The Red Ranger chose this place to face the Nighlok because the water in our world is more pure than that in the Sanzu River and it blocked Vulpes' view.

Just then, the Blue and Pink Rangers turned up to help. When they saw Vulpes, the Pink Ranger called Mike and Emily.

"Come on," Mike told Emily after taking the call, "the others need our help to fight a Nighlok over in Spring Valley."

What Mike and Emily didn't know was that the fish man was hiding behind a post and listening to every word.

"This sounds like a perfect time for my big moment," he said to himself when Mike and Emily had left.

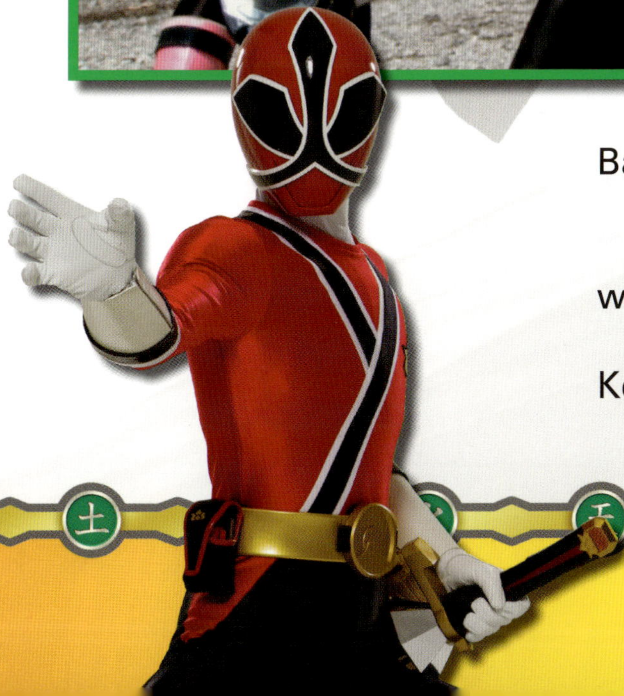

Back at Spring Valley, the fight was in full swing.

"Where are the others?" asked the Red Ranger.

"They were chasing the fish man, but they're on their way now," replied Kevin.

"Huh?" said Jayden, who didn't have any idea what Kevin was talking about.

"Try this spell, Fox Fire!" Vulpes yelled as he threw out a stream of fire at the Red Ranger, knocking him off his feet.

Luckily, the other Rangers arrived to help. They combined the force of their weapons, but Vulpes used his Fox Reflection Spell to turn the power of the Rangers' weapons back against them, and they were all flung to the ground.

天 木 火 水 土

Out of nowhere, a shower of Barracuda Bombs flew at Vulpes, knocking him over. It was the fish man!

"Now, this is a big moment. Man, this is going to be so golden," he announced.

The Rangers couldn't believe their eyes when the stranger pulled a gadget from his pocket.

"Samurai Morpher! Gold Power!" he shouted, and the Rangers were amazed to see the young man morph into a Gold Samurai Ranger.

"Gold is good to go!" he said as he stood before Vulpes.

The Samurai Rangers were stunned. They had never heard of a Gold Ranger before! The Gold Ranger readied himself to face Vulpes, but the Nighlok called upon a horde of Moogers to battle for him. Moving faster than the eye could see, the Gold Ranger dispatched the Moogers with the legendary Sheath Slash manoeuvre.

As the Gold Ranger continued to battle Vulpes by himself, the Red Ranger dived in to help. Combining their forces, they soon defeated Vulpes. When Vulpes came back moments later as a MegaMonster, the Rangers knew that it would take all five of them to wipe him out. Going into MegaMode, the Rangers combined to become the Battlewing Megazord and prepared to fight. But Vulpes still had some tricks up his sleeve.

"Fox Veil!" he cried, wrapping himself in a veil of invisibility.

"How can we fight him if we can't see him?" asked the Pink Ranger.

Just then, the Gold Ranger activated his own MegaMode and the Rangers were amazed to see that he had his own Zord – the OctoZord.

"Could this guy really be a genuine Ranger after all?" asked the Pink Ranger.

The OctoZord sprayed a cloud of inky mist and Vulpes was revealed. Then the OctoZord's tentacles knocked the MegaMonster off its feet. Now the Battlewing Megazord had a chance to strike with their Megazord's Katana Blade! Vulpes fell to the ground, defeated at last.

"Samurai Rangers, victory is ours!" said Jayden.

After the battle, when the Gold Ranger demorphed, Jayden recognized him at once as his childhood friend, Antonio. Many years ago, Jayden had given Antonio his OctoZord as a parting gift. Antonio had vowed that they would meet again, both as Samurai Rangers. All the Rangers agreed that Antonio had definitely delivered his golden moment!

The Blue and the Gold

At the Shiba House, Antonio, the Gold Ranger, was showing the other Rangers the ClawZord. Mentor Ji had hidden away the battle-damaged Zord for years.

"Mentor asked me to perform a bit of my tech-whizz magic," said Antonio, pleased to have this important responsibility.

As the Rangers stared at him, fascinated by the new Zord, Antonio reached for his Samuraizer and pressed a button to make Samurai symbols appear.

Antonio thought that showing the Rangers his hi-tech skills could help prove him to be a worthy Samurai Ranger. However, Kevin thought differently – Antonio was showing he was a computer nerd, not a Samurai.

"I know I wasn't born into the Samurai life like you guys, but I'm trying to help in my own way," Antonio said, realizing how difficult it would be to convince Kevin.

Later, Mike, Mia and Emily spoke to Antonio, and Antonio explained that he felt he had already proved himself in battle.

"Eat, drink, sleep being a Samurai. It's the only way to impress him," said Mike, knowingly.

From now on, Antonio knew it was his mission to prove himself to Kevin.

Down in the dark Netherworld, Dayu was telling Master Xandred that Octoroo was working on a big scheme, and if it worked, all Nighlok would be able to escape the Sanzu River for good.

"Huh! Good!" snarled Master Xandred. "If that squid brain can really pull it off, then putting up with that lame blabbermouth all these years will be worth it!"

Back in our world, Octoroo was looking down a dark well, deep inside a forest.
"Kiddies' eyes will be crying and Nighlok will have a place to get wet when they're drying!" Octoroo cackled.
The Nighlok Antberry then set out to steal children's toys, followed by a horde of Moogers.

At the Shiba House, Antonio was working on his plan to prove himself to Kevin. He planted tiny cameras around the house in order to spy on Kevin's every move. At the stroke of midnight, when Kevin finally tucked himself into bed, Antonio went to bed, too.

Meanwhile, the Nighlok Antberry was using his sneaky skills to steal every child's toy in sight. Antberry targeted Bulk and Spike, stealing Spike's favourite teddy bear mascot. The next morning, Bulk and Spike could see a trail of slime where the teddy bear once sat!

At the Shiba House the next day, Antonio was spying on Kevin as he prepared to go for a run.

"Training and more training. Everything precisely timed," Antonio said quietly to himself.

Antonio decided to follow him into the forest. Suddenly, an evil chuckle rang out through the trees, stopping Kevin in his tracks.

"Did you hear that, Antonio?" asked Kevin, a little way ahead of Antonio.

Antonio couldn't believe Kevin knew he'd been spying on him!

"So, why the spy cams?" Kevin asked, frustrated.

"I just wanted to see what a true Samurai does," replied Antonio.

Kevin explained that being a Samurai was the real deal – it wasn't like being in a spy movie. However, he knew that right now they had to work together to find out where the evil laugh was coming from.

Deep in the forest, Octoroo was looking at all of the toys Antberry had managed to steal from children.

"It's brilliant! By tossing exactly 30 beloved toys in the well, the sorrow it causes will make the river rise and fill the well once again!" said Octoroo, quickly instructing Antberry to get to work chopping up the toys.

Before the well dried up a while ago, it was the Nighlok's main portal into the real world. Octoroo needed to get it working once again!

Kevin and Antonio were perched behind a nearby rock, watching their every move. Reaching for his Samuraizer, Kevin tried to get hold of Jayden, but the signals were blocked. Suddenly, Octoroo struck the rock with a fiery blast, and Kevin and Antonio quickly morphed into the Blue and Gold Rangers. Octoroo had put up secret barriers, which had jammed their phone signals, so they were unable to get help.

"Time to enjoy my new toy! Sanzu slime!" shouted Antberry, as he blasted a sheet of slime over the Rangers.

"Hey! My blade's as slippery as an eel!" cried the Gold Ranger, unable to keep hold of his Barracuda Blade.

The Blue and Gold Rangers left their weapons behind and started to fight Antberry with their Samurai moves. But Antberry was too slippery for them to get a grip on!

Octoroo joined in by blasting them into the air. Then he unleashed the Moogers on them.

"Alright, Moogers, go finish those pests off!" Octoroo ordered.

Back at the Shiba House, the others were wondering where Kevin and Antonio were.

"I've got a bad feeling about this," Jayden told the others.

In the forest, Kevin still couldn't get a signal on his phone. With Antonio's arm now injured, he decided to fight the Nighlok alone. However, within minutes, Kevin was cornered by Moogers.

"Back off, Moogers!" shouted Antonio, coming to Kevin's rescue.

Antonio managed to take down the Moogers, but Kevin was annoyed that he had stepped in and put himself at risk.

"Being a Samurai is more than just following ancient traditions," Antonio said. "It's about being a warrior, a protector of all things good."

Kevin realized Antonio was right, and he had the true spirit of a Samurai. He told Antonio the other Rangers would turn up soon, as he wasn't at the house in time for practice.

As Kevin and Antonio reached the top of a slope, a wall of Moogers stood waiting.

"Take a deep breath, 'cause the battle's about to begin," said Antonio.

They quickly morphed into the Blue and Gold Rangers and went head-to-head with the Moogers, defeating the Moogers in seconds. Just as Antberry was about to chop up the first toy, the Rangers attacked, and the evil axe fell into the well.

"Even if you can hold your weapons, you can't slip away from me!" cried Antberry, knocking both Rangers to the ground.

Suddenly, a huge fire-strike sent Octoroo and Antberry flying. The other Samurai Rangers had come to the rescue!

The Red Ranger's blazing strike overpowered Antberry's sheet of slime, and quickly turned him into a fiery blaze. The Rangers' amazing Samurai moves then finished him off, sending him into the dark well.

Within moments, Antberry turned into a MegaMonster, ready to fight!

"MegaMode Power!" the Rangers shouted in unison.

The Rangers jumped into their Zord cockpits, joined by the Gold Ranger with his special OctoZord.

"Octo Spear Megazord! Armed for battle!" the Rangers cried.

The Megazord wasn't able to get a grip on the slimy Antberry, so they blasted out ice to freeze him. Then they used their electric spear to take him down for good!

When they returned to the Shiba House, all they had left to do was give back the stolen toys to the children.

"We get to make things right. That's the great thing about being a Samurai, right Antonio?" said Kevin.

Antonio had proven himself to be a great Ranger in battle and Kevin had finally accepted him into their Samurai team.

水 火 天 木 土 水 火 天 木

Team Spirit

One morning at the Shiba House, Mia, Mike, Kevin and Jayden were hiding from Emily, as they were preparing food and decorations for her secret birthday party the next day. As soon as Mia offered to bake a birthday cake, the others quickly explained that Antonio had ordered one already – her baking was that bad!

In the depths of the Netherworld, Octoroo noticed something was wrong with Master Xandred.

"He's like a stick of dynamite with a really short fuse! We need to be careful not to upset the big guy," Octoroo warned Dayu.

Meanwhile, Antonio was sitting on a riverbank, eager to catch a nice big fish for Emily's birthday. In a box behind him sat his injured ClawZord.

"She was so cool!" said Antonio about Emily, to his ClawZord. "And she accepted me right into the group from the start."

Then Antonio promised to have the ClawZord up and running again in no time.

In the Netherworld, Octoroo could see the Nighlok getting stronger and stronger as the Sanzu River continued to rise. Suddenly, the menacing Splitface climbed onto the boat .

"And I'll go scare those human crybabies to raise it even higher!" said Splitface to Dayu and Octoroo.

Meanwhile, Deker was in our world.

"Master Xandred's binds can't hold me," Deker said to himself. "But my cursed half-human, half-Nighlok existence still imprisons me. My fate is sealed."

As Deker walked, Antonio was walking towards him, pulling his fishing cart. Unaware of Deker's true identity, Antonio invited Deker to have a fish lunch with him. But Deker was on a mission, so he declined and walked away. Suddenly, Jayden called Antonio to alert him of a Nighlok attack.

In the city, the scary Splitface was already creating havoc. He was stealing people's spirits, causing them to fall into a deep sleep.

"I have such a sweet tooth for spirited snacks!" Splitface announced.

Just then, Splitface was targeted by a burst of electricity that immediately knocked him to the ground. The Samurai Rangers leaped into action against the Nighlok, but found Splitface impossible to fight once his body separated into lots of evil faces, which flew around them in a swarm.

Suddenly, Splitface cornered Emily, stealing her spirit and sending her into a deep sleep. Splitface then told the Rangers his evil plan.

"Her spirit was delicious! And in 24 hours, it will be mine forever," said Splitface.

Only if the Rangers defeated him would they be able to reclaim the stolen spirits. However, Splitface was heading back to the Netherworld where humans couldn't follow. And he wasn't planning on coming back! The Rangers had to think of something – they couldn't lose Emily forever!

At the Shiba House, the Rangers sat beside Emily as she lay fast asleep. Mentor Ji told them that Splitface had stolen the spirits of many other people.

"I can't believe by tomorrow night, Emily and all those people could stay asleep forever. We have to defeat that Nighlok before that happens," said Kevin worriedly.

"No matter what it takes, we have to save her," agreed Mike.

Meanwhile, Antonio had gone back to the park. He was determined to find a way to help Emily. Tapping the keys on his Samuraizer, he conjured his gold electronic Samurai symbol and threw it toward his ClawZord.

"Samurai symbol, live!" he shouted.

Antonio knew he had to get his ClawZord working again. To his dismay, the power of his electronic symbol failed to revive the damaged ClawZord.

Back at the Shiba House, Emily suddenly woke up.

"Thanks for putting on a brave face for me, but I know I'm not okay," Emily said quietly to her friends.

Within seconds, Emily was asleep again. Mike became angry and stormed out of the house, back to where they had faced Splitface earlier. Mike looked at the crack in the wall where Splitface had disappeared back to the Netherworld.

"You can't do this to Emily! Do you hear me?" screamed Mike, lashing out with his Spin Sword.

As soon as Jayden arrived, Deker suddenly appeared in human form. Deker realized that it wasn't the right time to fight the ultimate duel, so instead offered them a solution.

"There is one way for humans like you to enter the Netherworld. Simply trade your human existence to become a Nighlok. Willingly give yourself over to them and pass through the gap," Deker told the Rangers.

Suddenly, Deker transformed into his Nighlok form to show them he was living proof of this working.

Just as the team was about to throw themselves through the gap into the Netherworld, Antonio showed up. He explained a way he could draw Splitface back into the real world, using symbol power and his special ClawZord.

The Rangers lined up with their Spin Swords and hurled their symbol power at the ClawZord several times. The more power, the bigger the chance they had of finally activating the ClawZord. Suddenly, Splitface was transported from the Netherworld and appeared in front of them. It had worked!

The ClawZord threw a shocked Splitface against the wall and Antonio explained how he had brought him back.

"When we came in contact, I marked you with a symbol," Antonio told Splitface. "And after I finished programming the ClawZord, I just needed the other Rangers to help me activate it."

Jayden, Kevin, Mike, Antonio and Mia quickly morphed into Power Rangers to defeat Splitface once and for all. Now that Splitface was marked with power symbols, he could no longer separate the faces on his body.

The Red Ranger dealt a fiery blast with his mighty Fire Smasher. Just when they thought they had obliterated the Nighlok for good, he came back as a MegaMonster.

"Without Emily, we can't combine into a Megazord," the Pink Ranger said, worriedly.

But the Gold Ranger wasn't worried – he just needed to team up with his ClawZord to save the day.

The Gold Ranger jumped into the cockpit of his ClawZord and confronted the MegaMonster alone.

"Time to try out these pincer claws!" shouted the Gold Ranger.

Suddenly, giant Moogers rose up from behind the MegaMonster. The Gold Ranger targeted the Moogers with his giant claw spinners.

"Now for a big trick. ClawZord transformation!" instructed the Gold Ranger.

The ClawZord then transformed into the powerful Claw BattleZord East to take a few more Moogers down.

Then the Gold Ranger transformed into the Claw BattleZord West. However, the Moogers were shooting huge arrows at the BattleZord, and the Red Ranger knew the team had to step in and help. The Red, Blue and Green Rangers entered MegaMode and called up their animal Zords.

"Samurai Battlewing, we are united!" the three Rangers shouted in unison. The mighty Battlewing destroyed the Moogers and the ClawZord. The Gold Ranger then transformed into the strong Claw BattleZord South.

With the Claw BattleZord South's huge swords, the Gold Ranger fought against the MegaMonster.

"Double Katana, strike!" said the Gold Ranger, determined to save the spirits from Splitface.

But it still wasn't the end of the Nighlok. Calling on the Claw BattleZord East once again, the Gold Ranger defeated Splitface with its giant pincers.

Back at the Shiba House, Mentor Ji was sitting beside the sleeping Emily. Suddenly, a bright ball of light appeared and entered Emily's mouth, waking her immediately – her spirit had returned! In the nearby hospital, all the people were waking up, their spirits now saved.

"Samurai Rangers, victory is ours!" said the Red Ranger.

Once they all returned to the Shiba House, Mia took Emily to the others, where they were ready to give her a birthday surprise.

"You guys are the best," said Emily, as Mike presented her with a birthday card from her sister.

"No, Emily. Mike was right. You're the best. We're just so happy to see that you're okay. Today, victory really is ours!" said Jayden, happy to have his friend back.